Notice is hereby given that the author claim the full trade-mark rights to the all inferences of the "Reclaiming Black Wallstreet Imploring the Power of Service", "Black Wallstreet" "Reclaiming Black Wallstreet" utilized throughout the various books, tapes and any and all electronic media used to convey the Reclaiming Black Wall Street: By Imploring the Power of Service - Get Rich In Spite of Yourself.

Scripture quotations are from the KING JAMES VERSION of the Bible.
Printed in the United States of America

ISBN 978-0984973804
LCCN 2011945931
Reclaiming Black Wallstreet: By Imploring the Power of Service – Get Rich In Spite of Yourself

---

ATTENTION ALL ORGANIZATIONS AND GROUPS:

Quantity discounts are available on bulk purchases of this book for educational purposes. Special books or book excerpts can also be created to fit specific needs. For information Appletree Media Group, Inc. 1102 Santa Fe Trail, Suite 1, Duncanville, Texas 75137, www.spreadthatwealth.com.

This Book Is Dedicated To My Wife Margie R. King

For her constant support, encouragement and push for the completion of this project over the years. I would not have completed this work without her steadfast love and desire to see this project completed. Without hesitation I proudly admit that this is much more her accomplished project than mine "Reclaiming Black Wallstreet: By Imploring the Power of Service - Get Rich In Spite of Yourself", therefore –

Congratulations **Mrs. Margie R. King** for a job well done.

I Love You!

Foreword

What has been will be again, what has been done will be done again; there is nothing new under the sun. Ecclesiastes 1:9 (NKJV)

If I am to do justice with this Foreword, it must be prefaced with the above scripture. With that said I am eager to get on with my contribution for any enhancement I have to offer this book. The imperfect person I am, I am deeply rooted in my Christian faith with God being the anchor of all my endeavors; therefore I am compelled to witness so. Dr. Martin Luther King, Jr. said;

"The belief that God will do everything for man is as untenable as the belief that man can do everything for himself. It, too, is based on Superstition."

***The rich history of our ancestors' achievements, garnered through the provisions of serving people, I am thankful at this historic time [2012] to share in expanding the literary industry with this new title:* RECLAIMING BLACK WALLSTREET: BY IMPLORING THE POWER OF SERVICE - GET RICH IN SPITE OF YOURSELF.**

I'm impressed with the work of Louis M. Grafe and his book, GET RICH In Spite of YOURSELF; which inspired me to incorporate his title and most of his work in transformative ways, while addressing the

economic stagnation of Black people in mass. My prayers are this work will bring forth open minds and willingness to allow God's love and guidance to get Black people on track toward full employment, love of serving people in all phases of life. Close examination of Bible study has revealed the greatest commandment in Christian Law;

"'You shall love the Lord your God with all your heart, and with all your soul, and with all your mind. This is the great and foremost commandment. The second is, 'You shall love your neighbor as yourself.' On these two commandments depend the whole Law and the Prophets." Matthew 22:34-40

Giving the highest commendable recognition to Mr. Grafe's book; GET RICH IN SPITE OF YOURSELF, I recognized his following as the same teaching which had been earlier emphasized. Most of the same can be theorized as works of some very stately Black men of the past, one such person is Dr. Robert Russa Moton-1928 he stated;

"We must demonstrate our capacity to cooperate among ourselves, before, demanding any cooperation

where the resources of others are at stake. Business is the ultimate test of our ability to cooperate. Somehow we must learn this fundamental lesson. It will be costly; there will be some loss in the process, but we must keep it up until we have developed within the race a group of people of definite capability and unquestioned integrity, who can lead the way to larger achievements for the benefit of the whole race."

Mr. Grafe strongly opposed The Wall Street Stock Markets as a means of investments. In theory he was perhaps correct, however Adam Smith' "free market theories" were completely entrenched in the minds of American Consumers by his time. Currently, at this precise time, there are many different financial products/service instruments available on the market that is conflicting. Nearly impossible to differentiate using Grafe's position relative to Wall Street, Banks, Insurance Companies and other investment tools. This responsibility you will have to accept or entrust someone to be your financial caretaker. This is not a suggestion or advice as to any do's or don'ts relative to investing yours' or anyone's money seeking a return on investments.

This is a great book for us, in mass, to reexamine our works, values and the tools available to do good work, i.e. providing services for our kinsmen, communities, cities, states and our country. The instructions presented for us in our Christian Bible, serving God and his people are the only "DESERVING" ways. What ever method you choose should embrace ones that are moral, legal and Godly!

In these seasons of change it is imperative that people (we) examine all available information, historically and presently, then move aggressively to seek counsel with family, trusted advisors and friends in an objective manner. Giving back to your community is not always the noblest thing to do. Not taking away from our community is the highest order of nobility.

Chevis King, Jr.

A man to whom God has given riches and wealth and honor, so that he lacks nothing for himself of all he desires; yet God does not give him power to eat of it, but a foreigner consumes it. This is vanity, and it is an evil affliction. Ecclesiastes 6:2 (NKJV)

Introduction - Reclaiming Black Wallstreet ®

Have you heard of Black Wallstreet – Tulsa, OK? It's a dearly beloved question which I believe has reached talker's remorse due to it's over use. A well intended question hoping to produce a positive feeling about ones' historical prowess. I am guilty as anyone and my experience has been, from both ways, a feeling of compunction for having gone through it. Most of us love a good stimulating conversation, most of all, one where there is no doubt as to blacks having been victimized. Having read about Tulsa many times, I search mentally for answers and ask why such a thing happened, why a thriving commercial retail institution had to be demolished by local militias. After all they were law abiding African American citizens. What were their crimes emanating from Americas' jurisprudence? Was the real reasons economic jealousy due to the beginning of the Great Depression?

This book is intended to raise the level of discussion from talker's remorse to visions of historical accomplishments and feelings of future self-worth. I believe there exist within the African American mass a huge number of experienced capable people available and desirous for such an undertaking. What has been lacking is a well simple defined modus operandi' that surpasses "affirmative action" by deploying the same model used in Tulsa, Durham NC, Mound Bayou MS, Rosewood, FL and other places in America. I am convinced that victimology is a worthwhile undertaking and should be done concurrently with a coherent educational economic agenda, the most important element of the African American community. I am speaking of an economic plan that leads towards embracing capitalism with an escalation of retail service merchants, liking to that which happened with the aforementioned black communities such as "Black Wall Street" etc.

The emerging zeal for "Reclaiming Black Wall Street ®" I am feeling, has much to do with Louis M. Grafe' "Get Rich In Spite of YOURSELF." This book written circa 1945 is well crafted, in my opinion, for the needs of our time. The underpinning of Grafe' book is the spiritual reference to the command of serving your fellow man gives rise to its validity. It's well scripted manners of serving people both DESERVED and other UNDESERVED services are riveting.

The historical fact regarding the achievements of African American retail service providers, bears out the elements of Grafe' book and the claim can be made that the motivation of such a book was crafted from the success of many African Americans practicing the vestiges of "Black Wall Street" which personifies the book in its totality. The debate about the historical tragedy of Tulsa is not included in my book, "Reclaiming Black Wallstreet Imploring the Power of Service", should not divert the books' sole intent of redirecting our path toward a more perfect retail economic union.

The most important operative words in this writing are "economic plan." A Retail Economic Plan seems to be an anathema to some in black communities and for reasons unknown, notwithstanding "affirmative action", and heretofore those daring to bring forth such ideas have been cast persona non grata. However this is one undertaking I desire to participate in. I believe something nearing $50-$75 billion in retail expansion with increases of employment nearing 300,000-400,000 people in black communities nationally is an adequate benchmark as a start. This is not just a trial balloon; I am encouraging my readers to expect an announcement for such a plan forth coming during 2012 Black History Month.

The history aficionados will perhaps take issues with this book and I will say to "hold your power dry", I am in favor of rigorous debates relative to correcting the course of maintaining the small retail market share in black communities nationally - nevertheless African Americans' income continue to increase annually. We pray you will enjoy this book and recommend its reading to others, moreover offer it as a gift. In this season of participating in the available high tech experiences, I am inviting you to become part of a new expanding legacy by including the emergence of a renewed spirit of economic surges in your repertoire.

Table of Contents

RECLAIMING BLACK WALLSTREET:
BY
IMPLORING
THE POWER OF SERVICE -
GET RICH IN SPITE OF YOURSELF

CHAPTER I

FUNDAMENTAL PRINCIPLES

CHAPTER I - FUNDAMENTAL PRINCIPLES

Is there a Law of Success? There is. Can we learn what it is? We can. Why doesn't everyone already know it? Because it is "hidden from the eye or the understanding; secret; concealed; hence, mysterious, supernormal, or supernatural." Why don't successful men let us know what the law is? Because such men themselves do not know what it is; for a time, they simply live by it unconsciously.

There is nothing magic or hocus-pocus about it. I found the law in the Bible, the greatest of all mystic books, and the most authentic. I call this law of success mystic because you will not really understand it by merely reading the words. The words must be seen in a certain light before their real meaning dawns upon you.

In order to reach the proper viewpoint from which to see the meaning of the law, one must have a proper conception of money. As this book is designed for the unlearned as well as the learned, and must therefore be brief and to the point, I will not parade my erudition by giving the many definitions of money, but will confine myself to giving the one definition that I have found most useful in understanding the spiritual law of success. It is this:

Money is deferred service.

In other words, if you have money you can exchange it later for service of some kind. Your grocer will give you food for it, your druggist toiletries, your landlord the use of his property, which is accumulated service of the building trades plus the continuing service of the community. In short, all civilized community life is based on an exchange of service for service.

For example, if you need a new hat, you first give service to your employer (and incidentally his customers), for which he gives you money, which is deferred service. Then a merchant serves you by providing the new hat, and the money goes to him. Then a grocer serves the merchant, and the money is again exchanged. This goes on endlessly, the money passing in turn through hundreds of hands, each time for a service of some kind. Whoever happens to have the money has given a service but has not yet received a service in exchange for it. Whoever happens to have the money has service coming to him.

Herein lies the convenience of money--that by using it you can exchange service to one man for service from another. You do not have to do without a new hat just because the hat store does not need your service. Just so you serve somebody, others will be ready to serve you. You will be denied service only if you serve nobody.

Of course, if you wish, you can give service and receive nothing in exchange for it, neither service nor money. But in the long run you will find it impossible to live without service from your neighbors. You will be forced, eventually, to receive service in exchange for service, or to receive money in exchange, which amounts to the same thing.

All my readers, I believe, will now be ready for the first rule in the Spiritual Formula for Success. I saw it repeatedly in the Bible for many years before I realized its true meaning. As given there, the first rule is; "Whosoever will be great among you, let him be your minister; and whosoever will be chief among you, let him be your servant." (Matthew 20:26, 27.)

Finally it dawned upon me that this did not mean that I should drop the kind of work at which I was skilled and become a domestic servant, not that I should become a preacher. Either as a preacher or a domestic servant, I would probably have been the world's worst. I could do far more good in the world in my own profession. What it did mean was this:

SUCCESS RULE NO. I

> *"Whosoever will be great among you, let him minister unto the people's needs; and whosoever will be chief among you, let him give service in that field in which he is most skilled."*

Now that is not the whole of the Spiritual Formula for success. It is the first rule only. Even so, let us not accept it blindly. Do the great really become so by ministering to the people's needs? Certainly Washington, Lincoln, and many others became great that way. Certainly Henry Ford, in developing an automobile and a mass production system by which it could be offered to people at a low price, became great by "ministering unto the people's needs." The same is true of other great industrialists, as well as of your locally successful merchants and manufacturers. The more people they minister to, the greater they are. Washington and Lincoln ministered, not only to their contemporaries, but too many generations since.

But how about the "chiefs" among us, those who are not great, but still fairly successful? Do they become so by "giving service in that field in which they are most skilled?" Their service is often not to the masses of the people, I admit, but they do give service to a limited group or class. This is true of the successful small business men, the physicians, lawyers and other professionals, the superintendents, the managers, the artists, the writers, the educators, the purveyors of comfort or entertainment. If they attain any degree of success; they do so by giving service in the field in which they are most skilled. They may not become great, but they do rise above the common level, to become "chiefs" among us.

The domestic servant serves only a few people, the successful business man many. The latter, therefore, gives the greater service, and gains a greater reward. But the domestic servant is also giving service in that field in which he is most skilled. Why is not he also a chief? Why do many who try to minister to the people's needs fail to become either great or successful? Why do others become chiefs for a time, and then fall by the wayside? Rule No.I does not answer these questions. Evidently more rules are needed, and will be given later in this book. Meantime you have learned this:

Though following Rule No.I does not guarantee success, it is ONE of the rules that must be followed if you are to achieve deserved success.

You probably noticed that word "deserved." Is there such a thing as undeserved success? Unfortunately there is. It is the kind of success achieved, not through service, but THROUGH OTHER PEOPLE'S LOSSES, through DISSERVICE. It is the great misfortune of America today, the cause of nearly all our troubles, that men can achieve affluence (success is the wrong word) in such a manner. To illustrate, in gambling one man's gain is always another man's loss. It is not the exchange of money for service. And this holds true whether the gambling is in the pool room or on the stock market.

The big Wall Street fortunes, made by speculation, consist of the losses of hundreds or thousands of small investors, although of course the wolves sometimes take fortunes away from one another also. Making fortunes in this way would not be possible, of course, if the little operators were not trying to do the same things to make an undeserved fortune through DIS-service instead of service.

As nine out of ten men lose when trying to make money in this way, I shall not encourage you to try it. Many other forms of "trading", whether in Wall Street or Main Street, are profitable only through other people's losses. Even if I could, I would not help anyone to cheat the Law of Life in such a manner.

We can now proceed to the next rule in the Spiritual Law of Success. In the Bible I found two commandments which were said to contain all the Law and the Prophets. The first is outside the province of this book, but the second was "Love thy neighbor as thyself." Now most people understand this as meaning that we should just have a good feeling toward our neighbor, a kind of inward glow that is quite pleasant, a titillation of the emotions such as we all get when we look upon a beautiful child. I made the same mistake myself for a long time. But how does such a feeling compare with the average mother's love for the child? The one is idle fancy compared with the lifelong devotion of the other; the one is a smug and flattering pastime for leisure moments, the other stops at no sacrifice of toil or health or even life; the one serves self only, the other serves the beloved without stint and without measure. In fact, that pleasant feeling is mere delusion, make-believe, unless it is expressed through services, only then is it love.

Did the Good Samaritan simply smile kindly at the stranger in distress, sympathize with him, and pass on? No, he stopped to serve him. Love without service is no love at all; service is its only measure. Thoughts such as these led me to what I believe is the true meaning of that commandment above mentioned. It is this:

SUCCESS RULE NO. 2

"Serve thy neighbor as thyself."

I can hear some of my readers saying "What! That's nothing but charity; people can't get rich that way." But they can, and they do. I hope Henry Ford will pardon me if I mention him again; but I like to use illustrations with which even the humblest reader is familiar. Did he serve his neighbor as he would himself? I can imagine him saying to himself as he started out. "If I were a man of modest means, what kind of car would I like to have, what price would I be able to pay, how long would I have to use the car, how much up-keep expense could I afford?" Then he proceeded to serve his neighbor just as he would serve himself if he were in the same position. Only a man with whom service is a passion would supply parts for cars twelve and fourteen years old, as Ford does. I can imagine Ford saying to himself, “If I were a poor man, forced to buy an eight year old car at second or third-hand, in what condition would I want it to be, how long would I continue to need parts for it, how much gasoline could I afford to buy? “

Because Ford sought to serve this man also, his cars have had, most of the time, the greatest value in the used car field. I imagine this was a totally unexpected reward for the service he gave, automatically increasing the demand for new cars. Such unexpected rewards for service freely and eagerly given are what make men deservedly rich.

Compare the highly successful merchant in any city with his competitors who fail, or who drag along, without profit or growth, for year after year. The success has a high ideal of service-- a widely varied stock, smartly chosen; well trained employees; refinements to make the customer feel welcome and appreciated; policies that flatter and satisfy even unreasonable customers; products that are the very latest and best of their kind. This is the kind of service the merchant would want for himself, and this is the kind he gives his customers. He personally cares more for quality and refinement than price, would rather, himself, pay a fair price than risk later disappointment; he therefore serves his neighbor in that way.

On the contrary, the failure does just the opposite. He has a less varied stock, including inferior goods calculated to deceive his customers as to their vogue or quality; his employees are taught trickiness; his policies are selfish and niggardly with dissatisfied customers; his prices may be fair or even cheap on some items, but he makes up for it by exorbitant prices on others where the inferior quality is not obvious. If he were as unfamiliar with the tricks of his business as his customers are, he would not like to be served that way. Because he does not serve his neighbor as himself, his establishment remains on the ragged edge year after year, or fails altogether. As a merchant he is not a success, though he may make money on outside deals, trading to the loss of other people in the objectionable way I have already discussed, or he may go through bankruptcy, saving his own skin at the cost of his creditors. But any one who makes money through DIS-service is not a true success, no matter how large his bank account.

It must not be thought, however, that the high quality merchant success I have discussed is the only kind that follows rule No. 2. Another merchant may achieve equal or even greater success by abandoning many of the refinements of service I pointed out, by endeavoring to serve the humblest of his fellow-men by cutting down all items of overhead possible, by having only very economical merchandise with the smallest margin of profit possible. His is an honest service too, just the kind he himself would want if he were in his customer's shoes. He also follows Rule No. 2 and achieves success by it, though his establishment is quite different in appearance from that of the quality merchant following the same rule, and has an altogether different clientele. Rule No. 2 might be worded as follows, if such a wording makes it clearer to you:

Choose the clientele you expect to serve, and serve it as you Yourself would like to be served, if you were one of such a group.

It may be objected that most of us would like to be served for nothing, without any profit whatever to the merchant. But any merchant who tried that would be bankrupt in six months, and be UNABLE TO GIVE ANY SERVICE AT ALL.

None of us could get along very well if we depended for service on non-existent merchants. Civilized living requires EXCHANGE, either service for service or service for money; which is deferred service. No SANE man or woman can expect service on any other basis, except in cases of charity which, in the end, must be paid out of SOMEBODY'S profits. If profits are ever stopped, that will be the end of charity.

You do not have to be a merchant or manufacturer to follow the two rules already given. You can follow them in whatever job you hold. The employee of the merchant serves the customers just as the merchant himself does. The employee serves also his employer. He serves his wife and children by providing for them. When he spends his money he is serving those who depend on such spending for their living-- grocers, druggists, etc., together with THEIR employees. His wife serves by inspiring him to greater efforts, by making a home for him, by rearing his children.

Much of this kind of service is inescapable. It is the absolute minimum that God will permit without retribution. It cannot bring one complete success, though it may enable one to keep the wolf from the door.

But if service alone will not bring success, what more is required? For one thing, efficiency is required-- efficiency in service. That may seem to be a hackneyed word. In fact, all words that deals with the spiritual, holy principles of life are hackneyed, because they are INESCAPABLE. You face these principles at every turn in life; consequently you face also, at every turn, the words representing them. What is the parable of the ten talents but a lesson in efficiency? The obvious lesson is that it is God's commandment not only that we serve, but that we be efficient in doing so, that we do the utmost with whatever talents we have. The parable of the ten talents end with this quotation: "For unto every one that hath shall be given, and he shall have abundance; but from him that hath not shall be taken even that which he hath." Let me make it clearer by paraphrasing it for.

SUCCESS RULE NO. 3

"For unto every efficient one shall be given, and he shall have abundance: but from him that is not efficient shall be taken away all the talents and all the money which he hath."

This rule needs little discussion. Most of my readers will agree with it at once. Inefficiency usually leads to want and poverty, at least in the long run. Have you ever known a successful man who was not efficient at his job or in his business? (I am speaking here of genuine successes, not the traders who make money through DISservice.)

This may seem to be a hard rule for those who are naturally (or so they think) inefficient. But strange as it may seem, the Bible tells us how we may become efficient, how we may do so, not by tiresome drudgery, but with joy and enthusiasm.

Many people have the mistaken idea that efficiency is simply a matter of knowledge or experience. Too long have they believed that knowledge is power. The untrained, the uneducated, therefore think that efficiency is beyond them. But there are many men and women, highly trained, highly educated, who are not very efficient. The world, in fact, is full of educated failures. No, efficiency is not a matter of knowledge only, but a matter of feeling and spirit. Ponder these quotations from your Bible:

"Not slothful in business; fervent in spirit; serving the Lord." ROM.12:11

"Watch ye, stand fast in the faith, quit you like men, be strong." I COR. 16:13

"And whatsoever ye do, do it heartily, as to the Lord, and not unto men." COL. 3:23

In these quotations is the secret of efficiency. We must not only serve, but we must be passionately devoted to giving better service. Whatever we do must be done heartily, as if we are serving God instead of men. We must be fervent and enthusiastic, we must be watchful and alert to improve ourselves and our service. And all this must be done, not for an hour or a day, a week or a month, but for year upon year. How otherwise could we "stand fast in the faith," quit ourselves "like men, be strong"?

I can see my readers, right now, throwing up their hands and exclaiming, "But I am not built that way. I could never put forth such a prodigious effort. I cannot maintain fervency or enthusiasm all day long for year upon year." To tell the truth, no one can, UNLESS HIS FEELINGS ARE AROUSED TO A CONTINUOUS HIGH PITCH.

Even if you are convinced that success can be attained in no other way, you will not make the effort described, nor will anyone else (nor has anyone EVER done so) unless there is an intense and sustained feeling that drives him on, a feeling that never lets him rest unless he is up and doing. No intellectual reason, no amount of such reasons, no mere effort of your will alone, will enable you to persist in such an effort. BUT IF YOUR FEELINGS ARE SUFFICIENTLY AROUSED THE EFFORT BECOMES EASY, A JOY, THE NATURAL WAY OF LIVING.

Look into the history of any deservedly successful business and you will find that, in its beginnings, the men who built it devoted themselves night and day to nothing else. Their success was due, not to brains only, but to feeling, to great desire, to intense love of their work, sometimes to overwhelming greed for money or lust for power. These FEELINGS, whether good or bad, made the great effort possible. Success is not possible without fervency of spirit. Otherwise, even when we KNOW what should be done, we will not do it.

When our feelings are sufficiently aroused (not the mere surface ones, but the underlying moods that influence us day and night) we have what is popularly called DRIVE. We instinctively admire men possessing this quality, we instinctively feel that we should be like them, at least in some respects. We recognize that to such people success comes usually as a matter of course. As a matter of fact, however, the popular conceptions are wrong. These men do not have drive. Their indefatigable energy and alertness are not a matter of will. THEY ARE DRIVEN-- often in spite of the will-- by emotions that forces them into constant effort. This leads us to;

SUCCESS RULE NO. 4

One cannot DRIVE himself to success; one must BE DRIVEN by a dominant, constant, and enduring emotion or mood.

Without this dominant emotion, the best of resolutions, the most intelligent of plans, the keenest of inspirations, will never be carried out. The price of success is usually too high to be paid except under the influence of such a dominant emotion. Too many sacrifices, over too long a period, are required. We simply will not make them unless driven to do so by an exceptionally strong and long lasting emotion.

Emotions are really the result of our instincts. That is why they have so much power. The instincts behind them are a racial heritage-- THE DRIVING FORCES OF NATURE. They have resulted in the self-preservation of the individual and the continuance of humanity. It is foolish to go against them or to subdue them. The attempt often leads to futility or nervous breakdown.

The thing to do is to harness them, to direct them into desirable channels.

Our emotional life is not only highly complex but also highly contradictory. Various emotions pull in varying directions. There is fear and there is courage, greed and pity, love and hate, pugnacity and despair, love of home and wanderlust, ambition and laziness, joy and sorrow, self-pity and self-assertiveness, admiration and contempt, generosity and selfishness, desires of all kinds and other emotions too numerous to mention. There are sentiments, prejudices, inclinations, preferences—all names for varying degrees of emotion.

Little wonder, then, that few men have drive! Little wonder that they are changeable, vacillating, and lack determination. So long as these emotions are permitted to pull in various directions, efficiency is utterly impossible. Ask any psychologist and he will tell you that most of the failures and ills of mankind are due to CONFLICT OF EMOTIONS. Such conflict always results in inefficiency. Worry and anxiety, are an inevitable accompaniment.

We are concerned here only with the manner in which the conflict of emotion affects your efficiency. We can summarize our conclusions thus:

1. An inefficient person is one in whom no single emotion is dominant, the various emotions being in perpetual and serious conflict-- a person, in short, whose purposes are subject to constant change.

2. An efficient person is one dominated by a single emotion so powerful that other emotions are weak in comparison, or transmuted into servants or collaborators of the dominant emotion-- a person, in short, whose emotions work in harmony with one another to drive him constantly in one direction.

RECLAIMING BLACK WALLSTREET:
BY
IMPLORING
THE POWER OF SERVICE -
GET RICH IN SPITE OF YOURSELF

CHAPTER II

THREE GENERATORS OF SUCCESS

CHAPTER II - THREE GENERATORS OF SUCCESS

In the first chapter you were given a few fundamental principles upon which deserved success is usually founded. But there is a difference between knowing them and applying them. The mere knowledge that a dominant emotion may drive you to success does not automatically give you such a dynamo of power. Where and how can you attain it? Briefly, the answer is:

1. Choose the dominant emotion most likely to drive you to success.
2. Cultivate that emotion constantly.

In my own judgment there is one best emotion to choose. If I tell you right now which emotion that is, you may not agree with me. But if I name the other emotions first, pointing out their dangers and difficulties, you will soon see for your self that the emotion I have in mind is the only logical choice. So we shall begin with the emotions which sometimes lead to success, but which I do NOT recommend. The first of these is:

I. GREED OR LUST FOR POWER

Unquestionably one or the other of these is the driving force behind many apparently successful men. Usually, as in the case of Napoleon, Hitler and Mussolini, they overreach themselves and ended in failure. The history of these men does show, however, that a powerful emotion, even a questionable one, often leads to efficiency and temporary success.

But there is, in all of us, what cynics call the herd instincts, what psychologists call the social instincts, and what theologians call conscience. They inspire such feelings as pity, generosity, loyalty, patriotism, love, charity, tolerance and appreciation. They are deeply rooted, because Nature knows that men, without them, cannot live together and survive. These feelings clash with greed or lust for power, the conflict leading to vacillation, worry, indecision, fear, procrastination, laziness, or escape into non-productive activity. Few are the men so deficient in the social instincts that they can successfully make greed or lust for power their dominant motive. Hitler and Mussolini became insane, and I doubt whether modern physicians would consider Napoleon sane.

Do you think you could keep your balance if you deliberately cultivated greed or lust for power? The very distaste with which you contemplate the idea shows that emotional conflict and inefficiency would result. Only people already unbalanced can power their success with such a driving force.

II. FEAR OF POVERTY

This is the second emotion NOT recommended, though undoubtedly it is the driving force behind many moderately successful men. It leads many a man to learn a trade or profession, to work reasonably hard at his job.

But intense fear cannot be long sustained in the normal mind. It can inspire to a short burst of effort, but not to more. Where, in abnormal cases, the fear is sustained, becoming a dominant emotion, it has a paralyzing effect if not a calamitous one. Even a mild fear of poverty will cause worry, the postponement of decisions, unwillingness to venture, reluctance to make changes, dissatisfaction with the conservative course always followed. Mistakes of the past, the chances lost, together with the probable mistakes of the present and future, preoccupy the mind until the victim is hardly capable of decisive, courageous action or long sustained purpose. Nature designed fear as a useful emotion only in rare emergencies, when extreme danger makes a sudden burst of speed or pugnacity necessary.

It is quite a useful emotion when you are chased by a bull or must quickly dodge a speeding automobile; but no man ever achieved substantial success through fear of poverty. Another name for fear of poverty is;

THE DESIRE FOR SECURITY

It is the same old fear in milder form, and no mild emotion can become your dynamo of power. Only a strong emotion can drive you to success. The failure of most men is that this rather sickly emotion, the desire for security, is their chief motive for working. They are fortunate that conflicting emotions gain ascendancy most of the time, thus preventing its becoming an obsessing fear of poverty, with all its attendant evils.

Many men think they deserve credit because their ambitions are small, because their main desire is to avoid poverty and attain security. They even take a pious pride in their small ambition, affect a "holier than thou" attitude. Nonsense! Such men are unconsciously selfish. Is security their only purpose for living? How about serving their fellow-men, not in a limited or half-hearted way, but "fervent in spirit, as unto the Lord?" How about the more and better service, the utmost effort, which constitute their duty before God and man?

Fear of failure is akin to the desire for security. It has value only in emergencies. Many small business men keep going for years with the aid of this motive. An emergency arises, the fear looms; they work like beavers for a spell, even doing some hard thinking until the emergency passes. Then they fall back to their former uninspired, half-hearted efforts, more concerned with petty detail than with the achievement of more substantial success.

They are fortunate in that the fear cannot be maintained; they are unfortunate in that they have no better motives to inspire their efforts. Fear of any kind is ineffective in small doses, dangerous to sanity in large.

III. PRIDE

The third emotion among those NOT recommended as a chief motive for success is pride. This, too, is often the dominant motive in many moderately and temporarily successful men. Envy, the spirit of rivalry, the desire to "keep up with the Jones," undoubtedly inspires prodigious effort in some people and leads them to a success they might not achieve otherwise.

Pride need not be dispensed with altogether. As a complementary or subordinate motive, it has its uses. It often inspires the athlete in his training, the salesman in outselling other salesmen, the student in making better grades, the business man in beating rivals to new ideas and methods.

In the form of professional pride, it frequently inspires the scientist to labor indefatigably in his laboratory, the lawyer to win his case even for an impoverished or unappreciative client, the physician to show his utmost skill in a free clinic, the employee to turn in a workmanlike job in spite of meager pay and disagreeable conditions.

But the use of pride as a chief motive is dangerous. For short bursts of effort, as in an athletic contest, a lawsuit, a “drive” of any kind, it is stimulating. But for the long pull, pride, like the desire for security, is a coin with a reverse side-- fear of shame or humiliation. Cultivated continuously, pride would degenerate into this fear, with its accompanying worries, anxieties, conflicts of emotions. It would also turn into vanity, in which case fancied or exaggerated humiliations would keep its victim in a continual mental turmoil.

Such conflict and turmoil lead to changeableness and inefficiency. Certainly, therefore, pride is not the emotion to cultivate as the dominant emotion to inspire your life-long progress toward success.

RECLAIMING BLACK WALLSTREET:
BY
IMPLORING
THE POWER OF SERVICE -
GET RICH IN SPITE OF YOURSELF

CHAPTER III

FOURTH GENERATOR OF SUCCESS

CHAPTER III - THE FOURTH GENERATOR OF SUCCESS

We now turn from dominant emotions which I do not recommend, and consider a motive which I do. I doubt, however, that many of my readers can energize themselves with it continuously, without the support of still better generators of success. Though the motive is most effective and inspires some of our most famous men, it is difficult to cultivate to the necessary degree without special gifts or talents. The name I give this motive is;

LOVE OF WORK

By this phrase, I do not mean love of drudgery, or petty detail, or mere physical or even mental activity. I mean the love that finds its expression in creating, building or producing. I mean the love for expressing your highest capabilities through your work. In many fields it is called the artistic impulse. Psychologists call it the desire for self-expression, and maintain that none of us is altogether without it.

This is the motive that goads the great artist, the great scientist, the genius in all fields, to untiring and incessant effort. He is so inflamed with zeal that his work becomes a joy, an ecstasy. No sacrifice of toil or study or time, no sacrifice of self or others, is of the moment, if only the great work is forwarded. The same near-mania for his work, his business, his factory, energizes often the successful business man. His very delight in his work makes him unconsciously ruthless, to others as well as to himself. He is DRIVEN to success by the joy of creation.

As you can see, there is danger in such an impelling force. The man activated by it to a high degree is inclined to be unbalanced. His family suffers from his thoughtlessness, his community from his selfishness; he will brook no opposition, and will therefore take great hazards, both with the law and his fortune. As a result, he sometimes ends in bankruptcy, sometimes in the toils of the law, sometimes in domestic tragedy caused by neglect of his family.

Therefore, though I recommend love of work as a collaborating motive, I do not recommend it as the dominant emotion in driving you to success. True, success can never be achieved without it; but it can and should be subordinated to a less dangerous source of energy. Most of us, however, are not inclined to have such an overwhelming love for our work; consequently we can cultivate that valuable source of energy without fear.

Love of work, when balanced by superior emotions, is one of the greatest sources of happiness as well as success. What joy there is in expressing ourselves fully and completely through our work? The painters and sculptors are not the only artists.

The merchant is an artist in service, the salesman in selling, the foreman in handling his crew, the mechanic in handling his tools, the orator in swaying his audience, the auditor in preparing his charts and data sheets, the detective in tracking down the elusive fugitive.

The scientist, too, is an artist, in discovering and applying the secrets of Nature. All these enjoy exercising their skill, expressing themselves in their work, not only for the money thus earned, but for sheer love of it as well.

In the factory, the large office, the laundry, where many are cogs in a machine, the gratification of the artistic instinct is difficult. Nevertheless, those who rise to foremost positions manage to find some way of expressing themselves through their work.

One, assisted or driven by feelings of pride and rivalry, perfects his speed, until his production is greater than that of others. Another, often driven by strong curiosity, is constantly observing what other departments are doing, taking correspondence courses, inquiring about methods of competitors, perfecting his knowledge of all aspects of the business until recognition of his superior knowledge is inevitable.

Still another of these cogs in the machine is interested not so much in information as in human beings. Books and methods do not arouse his curiosity, but human nature does. He never tires of drawing people out, listening to their opinions, studying them. He gradually acquires an intuitive knowledge of human nature which enables him to influence people, to win their confidence, to inspire them to greater effort. The exercise of this skill gives him constant pleasure, for it is HIS means of self-expression. He is driven, just as any other artist is, to the constant improvement and use of his skill. Presently he is outstanding among his fellows, becomes a leader of the labor union, foreman or superintendent of the plant. He may be transferred to the sales department, become sales manager or vice president. Or he may be able to influence others to furnish the capital to start a new enterprise of which he himself is president.

The preceding paragraph is the story of thousands of men who have risen from humble positions to the presidency or general manager-ship of large corporations. Men of this type usually achieve success, for in them two powerful emotions are operating in harmony, love of work and love of people (love of service and love for their fellowmen). They are living examples of the rewards in store for those who follow the advice of the Bible to "be a servant" and to "love thy neighbor." The love for their neighbors may be unconscious on their part. They may think they are interested in their neighbors only for selfish reasons. But no man can drive himself to such constant study of and interest in his neighbors unless he subconsciously loves human beings. He may withhold any material gift to them, but he always gives himself. And his fellowmen, often, would rather have the giver than the gift. "The gift without the giver is bare."

A man of the type just described is an artist in human nature, an expert at soothing ruffled tempers, inspiring greater effort, winning confidence. He is a builder of harmony among his fellows, a producer of unity of purpose in his group, a creator of an atmosphere in which men are at ease. His is a subtle artistry indeed.

But we are beginning to encroach upon a motive which I have been reserving for another chapter: love of people. It is an even better emotion for driving you to success than love of work is; but for the time being, let us stick to the latter subject. Enough has been said, perhaps, to convince you that some phase of the instinct of self-expression has been operating in your own case, perhaps not with respect to your vocation, but certainly with respect to some avocation‹whether bridge or golf, photography or stamp collecting, gardening or reading about your favorite subject. The hobby or pastime that occupies your spare hours would be drudgery to many people. It does not seem to be work to you because of your emotional attitude. A mere change of your emotional attitude toward your job may be all that is needed to drive you to complete success, for then your job will be play instead of work.

Some of my readers may be inclined to think they have the proper love for their work, simply because they like to spend long hours at it. But by love of work I mean, not love for mere busyness, but a love for expressing the highest that is in you through your work. When there are big problems to solve, a genuine love of work does not permit their being set aside or dodged by the device of resorting to routine and unimportant tasks.

Many men use work as a mere escape mechanism, an escape from frustration, from heavy thinking, from facing the facts, from domestic or other troubles. They may work fourteen hours a day and pride themselves on their industry, but they are lazy nevertheless. They love only the easier work, and set aside the tough problems. They have no love whatever for tough brain exercise. Many small business men and farmers belong in this category, working hard physically, but refusing to bother their brains with keeping abreast of new methods and developments, changing conditions, etc. They do not love their work enough to be mentally alert for opportunities to improve it.

On the other hand, a far more successful farmer or business man may work only three or four hours a day. But in that time he tackles only the most difficult problems. And when not actually working, his mind is frequently turning back to those problems. He thus may get inspiration at any hour of the day or night. This man, like many successful executives, is impatient of detail and routine. Yet, because he has a genuine love of hard work, he is far more successful with his few hours of work than other men are with many. This man's work is not a mere escape mechanism, but an outlet for his highest faculty--the creative instinct. So don't judge your love of work by the hours you put in. Long hours may only betray a dislike for applying hard thinking to your work.

RECLAIMING BLACK WALLSTREET: BY IMPLORING THE POWER OF SERVICE - GET RICH IN SPITE OF YOURSELF

CHAPTER IV

A PROFITABLE HABIT TO ACQUIRE

CHAPTER IV - A PROFITABLE HABIT TO ACQUIRE

The proper kind of love for your work is an absolute essential to success. There is another essential which I consider even more important, but even so, love of work must be added to it. The other essential will be discussed in a later chapter. It will show how, if you can't love work for work's sake, you may learn to love it for the sake of something else. But first I need to discuss a habit that is not an essential, but which nevertheless is often useful in building up love of work to the degree necessary for moderate success. It is the habit of;

THRIFT

I do not recommend thrift for its own sake, but I do recommend it as a means of increasing your love of work. A steady growth of your bank balance is a perceptible indication of progress. It calls the acquisitive instinct, a most powerful one, into play. You unconsciously begin to plan ways and means for improving your work, so that you can earn and save more. Thus your love of work receives effective support.

The elder Rockefeller had a habit of giving away dimes as a lesson in thrift. He attached great importance to this habit, not for the sake of the few dollars accumulated, but for the sake of the inspiration, the uplift, it gives to your love of work. This is worth a thousand times the money itself.

Thrift is impossible without emotional support. No amount of so-called will-power will make you thrifty, without a supporting goad of some kind. For some people fear-- "prepare for a rainy day"-- is sufficient. But what a blight upon all inspiration it is to go through life in constant fear of rainy days ahead! What a danger to your psychological and spiritual health, your initiative, daring and freedom! It were far better not to be thrifty at all. People are instinctively right in rejecting such a motive for thrift.

Instead of this or any other negative motive, find a positive one to support your determination to be thrifty. There is always a desire to express ourselves through self-indulgence and extravagance. Unless you find a stronger desire by which it may be opposed, you will never be thrifty. I have no faith in will power whatever; it is desire that rules men. To oppose your desire to spend money, you might try cultivating a desire for a business of your own, or a home of your own, or a new automobile, or a library of technical books, a laboratory or workshop. But any desire that will cause you to save a nest-egg will do, such as a desire for travel, or moving to another city or state, or educating your children.

I know one young man who is saving money faithfully so as to go to a fashionable Florida hotel and live a life of luxury for two weeks-- a case where self-indulgence is made a supporting desire instead of a conflicting one. I encourage him, because meantime he is acquiring habits of thrift and his love of work is gaining great impetus. He works like a Trojan because the more he can earn the more quickly will come his day of dreams-come-true.

The inventor, the artist, the author, the exceptionally gifted man in any field, often do not need thrift to inspire a love of work. They cannot keep away from their self-appointed task. Geniuses are often thriftless, yet are successful nevertheless. But others usually find thrift useful in inspiring in them a love of work.

Thrift and industry have long been associated in the public mind, a universal recognition of the fact that thrift inspires industry. Did you ever hear of a successful farmer who was not thrifty? The farmer finds it easier than most of us to develop thrift, because the rewards are very tangible in his case-- a bigger barn, a new silo, or more hogs, cattle, etc.

He always has a great want which a short period of thrift can satisfy. The tangible rewards of his thrift are much more satisfying to his pride than the few additional figures in his bank book are to the city worker.

Moreover, the farmer's additions to his stock or equipment increase his output-- his efficiency-- thus increasing his pride in and love for his work. No wonder the farm lad often comes to the city and conquers where many city-bred men fail. He usually has better developed habits of thrift, and because of them, a greater love for work.

But remember that thrift is simply a means by which you may add to your love of work. If it becomes a dominant emotion instead of a supporting one, the acquisitive instinct leads to miserliness, greed, even crime; it leads likewise folly when, instead of relying upon your service to increase your savings, you turn impatiently to speculation, gambling get-rich-quick schemes, "playing the other man's game." Even if you should be one of the few persons who thus meets temporary success, you will fail because an over stimulated acquisitiveness never knows when to stop. The habitual gambler never becomes a good worker, and, if he lives long enough, always dies poor.

RECLAIMING BLACK WALLSTREET:
BY
IMPLORING
THE POWER OF SERVICE -
GET RICH IN SPITE OF YOURSELF

CHAPTER V

THE FIFTH GENERATOR OF SUCCESS

CHAPTER V - THE FIFTH GENERATOR OF SUCCESS

Again let us remind ourselves why we are discussing dominant emotions. Let us repeat the observations that brought up the subject. The first was

Success Rule No. 4:

One cannot DRIVE himself to success; he must be DRIVEN by a dominant,constant, and long-lasting emotion or mood.

In connection with this rule, we learned also that:

An efficient person is one dominated by a single emotion so powerful that other emotions are weak in comparison, or transmuted into servants or collaborators of the dominant emotion—one, in short, whose emotions work in harmony with one another to drive the person constantly in one direction.

Just think of the words most often used to characterize efficient, successful men; such words are energy, force, power, vigor, fervor, spirit, verve, dash, pep, fire, punch, vim, enthusiasm, zeal, ardor, vigilance, grit, stamina, determination, faith, steadfastness! These words do not describe intellectual qualities, but spiritual ones. They show a person's feelings rather than his thoughts. They are qualities of character; and character is determined by a man's dominant and permanent mood, his customary way of feeling rather than his way of thinking. In short, his feelings determine his thoughts; not that these do not stray sometimes, but they are always brought back to the same starting point and headed in the direction dictated by his dominant mood. If his dominating mood is self-indulgence, the gratification of every whim and fancy, he will never be a success.

We have learned, also, that certain emotions can, and sometimes do, drive men to success. These are:

1. *Greed or lust for power.*
2. *Fear of poverty.*
3. *Pride.*
4. *Love of work.*

So far as the first three are concerned, you are lucky if you are not dominated by them. Their cultivation would be dangerous. Only the fourth is recommended as a DRIVING emotion. If you have it naturally, well and good. Many geniuses or extremely gifted people do. But it is against ordinary human nature to love work for work's sake. The chances are you will have to love work for the sake of something else. The something else will then be your dominant emotion. What can it be? Though there are many other emotions which occasionally drive men to success, only two are so frequently effective as to deserve mention here.

These are:

5. *Love of people.*
6. *Love of God (religious zeal)*

At this point, I can see many of my readers lifting a skeptical eyebrow. What has religion to do with success? Who ever made a success by loving people? My answer is that the word "love" has a broader meaning than most people give it. If these skeptics will read through the balance of this book, I believe most of them will agree that love of people, understood in the light of its broader meaning, often DOES drive men to success.

For I maintain that the successful merchant serves people better usually because he loves them better. The successful salesman usually likes people so much that he must constantly be mingling with them. Everyone knows that, in most fields, being a "good mixer" is often an important element in a man's success.

Now a man cannot be a "good mixer" unless he loves people, at least to a certain degree. This liking for people, the desire to mingle with them, is love and nothing else. It may be of low degree; but it needs only the addition of a desire to serve people to make it a love of high degree.

The most widespread form of love is gregariousness-- the desire to mingle with our fellow-men. To mingle with our fellow-men is a fundamental need of human nature. Where this instinct is thwarted, the victim sometimes becomes an extreme introvert; inferiority complexes and other psychic ills develop; and these are often followed by physical ills. Seldom does such an introvert achieve success, though he occasionally does in certain special fields of effort.

But I do not accuse the introvert of not loving his fellow-men. He often does love them, is capable of, and sometimes makes, heroic sacrifice for humanity. But his love is inhibited, not given free expression, and he fails to reap the rewards of such love. Instincts, including the instinct of gregariousness, demand a sufficient outlet, and punish where the outlet is denied.

Gregariousness is the same instinct which holds sheep together in flocks, cattle in herds, wolves in packs. Man is not psychologically fitted for the secluded life. Nevertheless, most of the readers of this book will be introverts of greater or less degree. Most of them will be of a studious turn of mind, seeking to find in books a way to resolve the discontent, the emotional conflict, they sense within themselves, to find a cure for the inefficiency and failure these bring about, through any means EXCEPT the right one, the development of skills which will give adequate outlet to the gregarious instinct.

On the other hand, there will be a few readers of this book-- not many, because they are seldom studious and rarely read a book such as this, to whom the gregarious instinct is a handicap, interfering with their love of work.

These will be extreme extroverts, who in gregariousness seek ESCAPE from emotional conflicts arising from their work or other sources. Such men, if salesmen, dally in poolrooms, hotel lobbies or bars, instead of devoting sufficient time to calling upon, giving thought to, or serving their prospects and customers. Though they love people, their love is of low degree-- it includes no great desire to serve them.

RECLAIMING BLACK WALLSTREET: BY IMPLORING THE POWER OF SERVICE - GET RICH IN SPITE OF YOURSELF

CHAPTER VI

AN UNPROFITABLE HABIT TO AVOID

CHAPTER VI - AN UNPROFITABLE HABIT TO AVOID

In the last chapter, we by no means finished our discussion of the fifth generator of success-- love of people. But it is rather difficult to cultivate this emotion to the proper degree unless we first learn simple gregariousness, the desire to mingle with people. For the benefit, therefore, of those readers who are not "good mixers," we must defer more advanced aspects of our present theme until we have seen what can be done about this unprofitable habit of excessive introversion. Certainly this is a handicap because we cannot rise very far, cannot give our most effective service, until we can influence and win the liking of our fellow-men.

Even in the factory we cannot rise very far unless we develop the ability to handle men. No matter how much ability we have, we often cannot "sell ourselves," cannot get the opportunity to use our skills frequently and effectively. From newsboy to bank president, the man who can sell himself usually gets the job. The good mixer may fail, but at least he gets opportunities.

We have one advantage to begin with, however. We have habits of study, and are usually better read than the extrovert is. Also, we need not fear the dangers arising from overindulgence of the gregarious instinct. But we must set about the development of social skills in order to persuade other men to give us the opportunity to show our abilities.

It is the Bible's command to "love your neighbors", and this cannot be done effectively unless you mingle with them freely, learn to know them intimately. But this is not a matter of religion only-- it is a matter of efficiency, of mental balance, of a well rounded and successful personality.

It is a need of your nature that this love should find expression in daily and effective contact, in daily deed instead of the wishful thinking of the introvert. To be effective in almost any walk of life, you must have the inspiration of frequent and adequate communion with individual men and women, or you suffer and your work suffers.

SUCCESS RULE NO. 5

People will distrust what you offer them unless what they feel is that you are one of them, familiar with their daily life and problems, even their weaknesses and foibles.

A similar distrust is the cause of the general lack of success of many highly intellectual men. People do not feel that such men are of their own stripe. Such men are always suspected of not knowing and therefore not liking ordinary human beings. People are always sure the "good mixer" who likes them will give them better service than the introvert will. The latter has a hard time getting his service accepted anywhere, no matter how superior it is.

So we, in our search for success, are not going to be introvert Pharisees, thanking God that we are not like other men. We are going to mingle with the publicans and sinners, the Samaritans of our day. We are going into the highways and byways, to the weddings and feasts, to high circles and low. And we shall start with the knowledge that we too, being poor mixers, are sick; that we need the love of these people as much as, indeed more than, they need ours; that they, unconsciously perhaps, will render us a greater service than we can ever return.

The first thing that will surprise us is that we are not particularly welcome. We have not loved these people enough to learn how to entertain, to understand, to interest them. They probably look upon us as a "wet blanket." We hardly know their language, we are unskilled in their pursuits, we are unaware of what is going on. Because of our own ignorance of many details of their lives, their jokes pass over our heads. It is as hard for them to entertain such apparently stupid people as ourselves as it is for us to amuse or interest them. Because they are more socially skilled than we, their politeness exceeds our own, they hide their embarrassment, do their best to put us at our ease, either by letting us alone or making apparently a too obvious effort. Finally their embarrassment causes them to avoid our society.

After a few rebuffs, the introvert usually returns to his former habits with relief. He accepts the conclusion that the situation cannot be remedied. He is simply too little interested in his individual fellow-men to make sufficient effort. What can we do to avoid his course, to make ourselves welcome among average people, so that we may learn from and later serve them better?

Undoubtedly we shall have to do many things we do not like to do, at first. And we shall not do them unless we are driven to do so by some feeling. Perhaps you can arouse your pride. Are you going to let yourself be licked by this problem? Perhaps you can arouse your anger-- at yourself and your own in capacities. Or perhaps you will have to call upon the sixth generator of success which we shall disclose in a later chapter. We know that we cannot depend upon mere will power, unless there is some other strong and enduring emotion behind it to DRIVE you to do disagreeable things. Take your choice of the dominant emotions named in this book, or find some other, but a DRIVING FORCE for you must be found somewhere.

Having selected the one you prefer, USE IT to drive you to carry out the program which follows:

To begin with, we shall go everywhere we can get opportunity to converse with and make friends of people-- to church, or to lodge, or to meetings. At church, we shall take part in all activities possible. Perhaps we shall join a political club, perhaps groups furthering some other kind of purpose.

Many are anxious for members. After we join we shall feel like the stranger at the feast. But we shall keep on, no matter how long it takes, until the strangeness wears off. We cannot pick and choose our friends until we develop some social skill. We must be grateful to any group that gives us opportunity for practice.

But in any social group action as well as presence is necessary. Perhaps you cannot tell a joke. What is to prevent your learning how? When you hear or read a joke that appeals to you, go over it before retiring that evening, tell it to your reflection in the mirror, mull over it until you can give pleasure in retelling it. Do the same thing with interesting or humorous incidents you have experienced. Good story tellers are always mulling over their stories when alone--that is the secret of their success in this field.

You can do consciously what they do unconsciously. Your early attempts may be dismal failures. But with practice you will acquire greater skill.

People do not become socially acceptable without the sacrifice of a certain amount of time and effort. Sacrifice a little of your time therefore, to learning some sport, whether billiards or bowling, bridge or tennis, golf or fishing. Sports are a perpetual topic of conversation. Sacrifice some time, also, to learning how to dance. Learn about other subjects of interest to your group, at least enough to make your conversation interesting and your society acceptable. If you really want friends, you will make the effort. If you really have sufficient love for ordinary people, you will make considerable sacrifice to become pleasing and companionable to them.

But what about my reading? my study? you may say. Little good these will do you if you do not develop a personality which renders your service acceptable. Most introverts should sacrifice at least a year to their social education, and even after that year, should keep in practice.

Otherwise ordinary people will look upon them with suspicion and will not accept their offers of service.

Let me warn you, however, not to seek social outlet exclusively among other introverts, or with what you consider superior groups. You will then be in a class apart, still unfitted for intercourse with ordinary human beings, still unable to converse with them acceptably, still unable to render one service people demand usually before accepting others--that you put them at their ease, make them comfortable and happy.

After you do this, they are highly interested in whatever service you may offer. Until you learn to love and mingle with the usual run of people, you will be lacking in the social grace often necessary to success. Seek to enjoy, learn from, and serve "the least of these, my brethren."

Instead of looking upon simple gregariousness with contempt, as many do. I believe it an absolute essential to the development of a greater love. How can a man pretend to love when he dislikes mingling with his fellows? Genuine love wants to mingle, to touch, to commune with its object. If you love, you must like your fellowmen as they are, with all their faults and foibles-- though such liking does not preclude your hoping for and working toward their improvement.

RECLAIMING BLACK WALLSTREET: BY IMPLORING THE POWER OF SERVICE - GET RICH IN SPITE OF YOURSELF

CHAPTER VII

THE SECRET OF SUCCESS

CHAPTER VII - THE SECRET OF SUCCESS

They say that fear feeds upon itself, and grows abnormally. Love, too, feeds upon it's self and grows. Beginning with simple gregariousness, the growth of a higher form of love is natural and easy. But, unlike fear, love cannot grow abnormally. Love is the normal state of being, the state that puts you into entire harmony with all the laws of God and Nature, gives wings to your thoughts, inspiration to your efforts, and success to your enterprises.

Having practiced gregariousness until you like your fellow-men as they are, what is your next impulse? The first impulse of all love is to make the beloved happy. It is natural, therefore, that as your love increases, so does your desire to make people happy, until you will gladly make any sacrifice necessary to that end. To serve them day and night, to make yourself fit and ready for such service, to put into this mission the highest and the best that is in you, will then become the natural way of living. It will not be drudgery, but a joy. You will be unhappy if you are NOT serving your fellow-men to your utmost, doing your best to make them happy. You will thus be DRIVEN to success.

The preceding paragraph contains the spiritual secret of success which I promised you at the beginning of this book. Let us call it:

SUCCESS RULE NO. 6

Cultivate a love of people until your greatest desire is to make them happy. When this desire becomes an enduring passion for serving them, you will be DRIVEN to do everything necessary to success.

In short, only those passionately devoted to giving more or better service, always to more people, can ordinarily expect success; and such devotion can best be inspired by love for the people to whom the service is rendered.

Here is the dominant emotion we have been looking for, the one that is without danger to your mental well being, the one that is in harmony with every law of God and man, the one that can subordinate conflicting emotions which otherwise lead to inefficiency, and the one which will supply the driving force necessary to long continued application and inspired effort.

As with the other rules, let us weigh this one and see if it is confirmed by the histories of successful men. Consider, for example, a typical case of two singers. Both have a talent for singing popular songs, both have equally good voices for this purpose, though poor voices from the standpoint of a musical critic. With their mediocre talents, neither should ordinarily be expected to make a success.

One never gets anywhere. He sings chiefly to suit himself. He desires success, but does not love his audiences. His first thought is to show what a fine singer he is. The audiences sense his attitude and give him a frigid hearing. His failure is complete and final.

The other singer loves his audiences. His foremost thought is to make them happy. He sings the songs they like in the way they like them. In his desire to increase the happiness of his audiences, he is forever and keenly studying them. He notices immediately if any one of his mannerisms pleases or displeases. He is constantly trying to determine from individual acquaintances and from different audiences, how the public likes best to have its songs sung to them. He mingles with people constantly; first, because he loves them; second, to learn their likes and dislikes in the matter of singing. He may starve for years, while he is learning what his beloved people like, but nothing can discourage him. After years of trial and error, of love so great that he cannot give up, the audiences begin to recognize his love for them. They begin to listen with respect, then eagerness, then delight. Here, they think, is a man like us; he knows us and is one of us; he knows what we like and likes it as we do. He likes us; therefore we like him. There is a warmth of feeling in his songs which other singers lack, so far as his kind of audiences are concerned. Suddenly this singer becomes famous, a great success.

And the successful singer had no more to begin with than the failure Had-- far less, indeed, than many who never succeed -- except a long sustained, never to be denied, love for his audiences, and, therefore, a dominant emotion which finally drove him to making the long continued sacrifices necessary to success. Here you begin to perceive the secret behind the success of many radio and stage singers. The love for their audiences is often unconscious. Most successful singers of popular songs will give credit to their voices instead of their love, even when their voices are faulty from a critical standpoint. And we can forgive them this vanity so long as they love us. No one who disliked people, or was indifferent to them, could possibly make the effort and sacrifice necessary to success in this field.

In the above parallel, we could substitute two actors for the two singers, two writers of plays or novels, two builders of homes, two restaurants owners, two filling station owners, two merchants, two manufacturers, two salesmen, two preachers, two lawyers, two physicians, or almost two of anything else. The success is usually the one who loves his public or his clientele and is passionately devoted, therefore, to giving better service or to making that clientele happy.

It must not be thought that love for people can be cultivated only through social activities. It can be strengthened in the ordinary contacts of your business or employment. The merchant mingles with the customers in his store, the executive with his employees, the salesman with prospects and customers. Each through constant association, learns to love his clientele, to enjoy making people happy through his service, and, if he is to be a success, to devote himself passionately to the finding of ways and means by which ever increasing numbers may likewise be made happy.

Some men and women can cultivate such love for people even through correspondence. A successful mail order man once explained his methods to me as follows:

"It isn't what I say in my circular letters, my advertisements, my broadsides and booklets, that counts. Competitors can use the same arguments I do. It is simply that I am just an ordinary dub, no better and no worse than my customers, with the same failings they have. I like my prospects and customers because they are exactly like me. I have read thousands of letters from these people in the course of my lifetime, I have written thousands of answers, I have seen how they respond to my answers, until I know them almost as well as I know myself. In my sales copy, people can sense, between the lines, that I know them, understand them, like them; and that I am just the same kind of person they are. They respond by liking me, having confidence in me, preferring to deal with me. It is something intangible in advertising copy, like style and tone and personality—not alone sales arguments--that produces results. "I have noticed the same intangible something in the copy of other repeatedly successful mail order men. They are never highbrows, never superior men; but they are human, they have, somehow, somewhere or other, corresponded with thousands of ordinary folk, learned thus to understand and like them. And it can all be read between the lines in their copy."

In almost every field of activity, it could be shown that the successes are usually those who understand their clientele, who like them, and who are single-mindedly devoted to making ever increasing numbers of people happy through the service they render. Of course, they like to make money, but nearly all of them will admit they "like the game more than the money." And most of them, when they retire from business, are unhappy and bewildered because they are no longer serving the people they love.

Let us not, however, condemn the genuine artist, who is animated by love of work for work's sake instead of by love of people. The academic preacher, the classical musician, the aesthetic dancer, the painters and sculptors, the architects and the poets who adhere to artistic ideals and disdain any effort to please the populace, are much to be admired. They have deliberately chosen the hard way; the way which is seldom self-supporting, but depends upon the whims, the subsidies and patronage of the charitably or egotistically wealthy. And if they have genius or exceptional talent, it is the right way--art for art's sake, or science for the sake of science, or scholarship for the sake of scholarship. For them, love of work, by itself, is sufficient as a dominant emotion to inspire the prodigious sacrifices of time and effort necessary to success. But such people arc few and far between. And it is well known how egotistical, how cruel and selfish, great artists often are, in spite of their indifference to money. Nevertheless, such people are greatly needed to hold aloft the torch of artistic and scholarly ideals. If that is your task, and you have sufficient love of work, fulfill it by all means. You may be able to dispose of your wares by forming a partnership with someone who does love people and thereby achieve success; but usually this course means martyrdom.

Most of us, however, must be content with taking a little knowledge, a little skill or talent, and using them to the best of our ability for the purpose of spreading a little happiness to the multitude. By serving the many with our little talent, we are of as much use in the world as those who serve the few with a great talent. Our course is by far the more profitable; hence there is no reason to regret our lack of great talent, unless we fail to follow Success Rule No. 6, given in this chapter. But we cannot follow

Rule No. 6 long before we, too, become artists--artists in human nature, adept in pleasing the public, masters in serving them as they like to be served. We, too, then acquire love of work for work's sake, as a strong supporting emotion, though love of people is still dominant. When that combination takes hold of us, nothing can stop us, in the long run, from achieving success. We are DRIVEN to it by feelings that never let us rest until our purpose is achieved.

I do not wish to imply that all successful men are angels, animated by love and nothing else. Theirs is too often a low degree of love spread to many and no great love for any. Though the chief mainspring of their success may usually be love of work; that low degree of love for the many is an essential of the first magnitude as a supporting motive. Successful men, in spite of all their faults, DO like people; otherwise they could never give to their fellow-humans the attention and study necessary for success.

I have seen an Irishman, a very capable salesman, devote an hour to making an old lady happy by practicing upon her his Irish blarney. There was no motive in it, except that he liked to make old ladies, as well as everybody else, happy. Because he liked people, he was forever doing it. Nevertheless, he was quite a humbug. He would, without qualm, devote the same charm to selling you something of little value at an exorbitant price. Yet if he had not, fundamentally, liked people, he would never have been able to acquire his skill in blarney. Because his love never increased to the point of desiring passionately to serve people, it was sufficient only to make a moderately successful salesman of him, never a great success.

A man's love must be greater, must amount to a passionate devotion to giving more or better service, as described in Rule No. 6, before really great success can be expected. His love of people must be so great that love of serving them naturally follows. He must be as loyal to his ideal of service as the artist is to his artistic ideals, and as passionately devoted to it.

Nearly every great success involves sacrifice and prodigious effort possible only to a man dominated by a strong and long-lasting emotion, usually a love of people that attracts them to him, and a strong devotion to serving them that never lets the man rest. Most successes are far more interested in building a bigger and bigger enterprise, and thus serving more people, than they are in merely making money. They hardly realize they have any ideals at all. But when they say, as they usually do, that they "like the game more than the money," they are betraying a love of people and a desire to serve them, the more admirable because it is unconscious love. Most of them serve far more people, do far more good in the world, than the professed and conscious reformers and idealists.

Sinners though they profess to be, they are, all unaware, obeying that fine injunction of the Bible.

"With good will doing service, as unto the Lord, and not unto men."

And they are usually doing it, as the Bible recommends, "unto the least of these, my brethren." They are the prime movers in that exchange of service for service which makes civilized living possible. Their daily business is feeding the hungry, giving drink to the thirsty, shelter to the stranger, clothing to the unclad, cheer to the sick, entertainment or relaxation to the worried, transportation to the weary, inspiration to the confused, or making people happy through a multitude of other services. They are the greatest artists of all, the artists of service.

RECLAIMING BLACK WALLSTREET: BY IMPLORING THE POWER OF SERVICE - GET RICH IN SPITE OF YOURSELF

CHAPTER VIII

THE SIXTH GENERATOR OF SUCCESS

CHAPTER VIII - THE SIXTH GENERATOR OF SUCCESS

In preceding chapters, we have discussed all but one of the dominant emotions most likely to give you the "drive" necessary to success. Some are objectionable, some are dangerous, some are impractical for nine men out of ten. But there is one dominant emotion, not objectionable, not dangerous, and practical for every man or woman who is inclined toward religion. It is religious zeal, or love of God. If you are not religious, your best reliance is "love of people," but if you are religious, your "love of God" may be even more effective, if you learn to put "religious zeal" into your daily work.

We know that divided loyalties can tear a man to pieces, can arouse an emotional conflict which makes efficiency impossible. But just as divided loyalties can wreck a man, an UNDIVIDED loyalty can give him, indeed, God-like strength and power. Then we have a Joan of Arc, a Lincoln, a Garibaldi, a Florence Nightingale, a Moses, a Paul the Apostle. The way to a completely inspired, a completely successful life, is to lose all sense of self, to surrender ourselves completely to a Great Loyalty.

Such surrender puts the greatest force in the Universe behind your efforts. Laziness becomes impossible. Emotional conflicts, interfering with your efficiency, dissolve. Indecision, vacillations are swept aside.

You become a MAN WITH A MISSION. All emotions fall into line to support the great emotion. Complete harmony, the strength of an integrated personality, follow. Your progress is as impossible to stop as that of a great river.

If we are religious, the simplest of all courses for us to take is to lose ourselves thus; it is often the shortest road to success. It inspires the greatest effort, results in the greatest deeds, and gives the most complete happiness. We no longer have to drive ourselves to do the things necessary. We may be tempted by vistas along the shore; but we cannot stop we cannot deviate from our course. We are driven irresistibly forward in the main stream of life itself, achieving distinction and success main stream of because these are necessary to the Great Plan of our Creator, because we ourselves become important factors in the Plan, an essential part of the Driving Force.

The Bible makes it plain, as the quotations already given in this book indicate, that only by serving your fellow-men, as the Good Samaritan did, can you seek the "kingdom." Your service to the "least of these" is a service to God. If you adhere to a religion, your daily work, your job, through which you serve your fellowman directly or indirectly, should be made a part of your religion, should have religious fervor put into it, should become the supreme mission of your life. If your work is a service, that is easy. If it is a DISservice, find another job or another business, and then seek the Kingdom, using service as a vehicle. You need not worry about money. That also will be among the "things added unto you." And you will accept that money, not because you are greedy, but because it enables you to CONTINUE your service because its accumulation enables you to give more service to more and more people as the years go by, because you intend to use it as a faithful steward in establishing and maintaining the Kingdom.

SUCCESS RULE NO. 7

> ***a.*** *(For Religious people only) To do your best, in giving service to your fellowmen, is a duty you owe to your God.*
>
> ***b.*** *(For all others)*
> *To do the same thing is a duty you owe to yourself-respect.*

You cannot attain success unless you are zealous in the pursuit of it. Which is to be preferred, for your happiness and your sanity--to be zealous in your greed, your vanity, your lust for power, your fear of poverty or other base emotions which sometimes drive men to success; or to be zealous in your love of and your consequent service for either God or your fellow-men?

"Seek ye first the Kingdom" was good advice to those seeking success. But you must not interpret the advice as requiring you to search far afield, to leave your workaday life and lose yourself in mystic contemplation, or to go up and down the land lecturing and preaching. It requires you merely to "serve your neighbor", to love him, to do so to your utmost, to perfect your skills for serving people and serving always more of them, in whatever trade, profession or calling may suit your talents.

RECLAIMING BLACK WALLSTREET: BY IMPLORING THE POWER OF SERVICE - GET RICH IN SPITE OF YOURSELF

CHAPTER IX

THE BLUEPRINT OF YOUR CAREER

CHAPTER IX – THE BLUEPRINT FOR YOUR CAREER

The spiritual formula for success is now before you-- obscure perhaps, as such matters usually are; ill-expressed perhaps, because I am a business man, not a professional author. To be a success, simply live according to the principles outlined in preceding chapters, formulate a program based upon them, and then STICK TO IT. Write out the program, and read it every day, as refreshment for your memory and inspiration for your work. The sticking is the hard part, as with all programs; but I have pointed out certain aids which should make it easier than you have found it heretofore; the chief of which, is the cultivation of an abiding passion for serving your fellow-men to the utmost.

The average reader can make his own blueprint better than I can. But some readers will remain unconvinced or half convinced, and will not trouble to make a program unless someone does so for them. Most readers will no doubt disagree with my program, but in revising it they will be doing just what I want them to do‹making their own plan, better adapted to their own particular talents and circumstances, or at least more acceptable to their own particular psychology and more likely, on that account, to be followed.

The following course of action, therefore, is just a suggestion to stimulate your own thinking. Get some paper and a pencil, and, as you read, modify each step to suit yourself and your particular talents. When finished, you may experiment by changing the order of the different steps. The finished product will then be your own blueprint, upon which you can build with far more enthusiasm than you could upon mine.

STEP I. If you are not now serving the public or a part of it in some way, start doing so at once.

Nearly everyone earning money, whether at a job, in business, a profession, or in almost any other way, is already serving, a fact which shows the fundamental necessity for this step. So Step I is chiefly for the unemployed, the youth seeking his first job, or young people still going to school or university. Can they serve in the meantime? Yes, in several ways:

(a) by choosing the field of service in which they are most likely to serve best. (The classified telephone directory in any large city will show many fields of which you may never have heard);

(b) by preparing themselves for efficient service in that field;

(c) by learning to know people, through habits of gregariousness, so that they will better know how to make people happy;

(d) by quietly practicing the art of making people happy whenever opportunity offers, in conversation, sports, in the classroom, the home, the dormitory, the fraternity house, or elsewhere (making people happy is the main purpose of all service);

(e) by serving continuously, on committees, as an officer of a group, or by just being a good worker in your club, school, church, lodge or other organization;

(f) by joining other organizations or mingling with people outside of your particular group, where you may learn to know, love and serve other people, average men and women, whom some day you may serve in a larger way because of your increased understanding and love for them;

(g) by becoming acquainted with and mingling with the people you expect to serve in your later career, for the better you know them the better you will be able to serve;

(h) by helping your neighbors in every way possible (invent a way if none offers).

As we have learned, people will not accept the service you may later offer unless they feel that you know them, understand them, and are one of them. The foregoing suggestions are not sheer altruism, therefore, but a necessity if you are later to be a success in having your service ACCEPTED.

STEP II.

(a) If you have a job, business, farm, trade or profession, and are now working at it, step up your service by improving or changing it, by speeding it, by expanding it to reach more people, or by study and practice toward doing these things in the future.

(b) Meantime, devote considerable effort to making your associates, clients, customers, superiors or inferiors more contented and happy, an additional service anyone can undertake, which all can improve.

This step is necessarily vague, because there are so many kinds of jobs and services open to our readers. Write out your own Step II in detail, changing it to suit your particular walk of life. A difficult problem confronts the member of some labor unions, where union rules prohibit more than average production. But it is certain that the member will not make his fellow-workers happy by violating the rules. The member should therefore concentrate upon (b), also on study and practice toward obtaining a higher position or another job where his service will not be limited, or still better, on steps toward going into business for himself. He certainly cannot become a substantial success unless he finds some way to give more and better service to more people. A similar problem confronts the young professional man, the beginning lawyer or dentist who may want to serve more people, but who must wait for them to come to him. In a way, he lacks a full time job, and can continue to apply the details under Step I. In addition, he can gain skill and a better knowledge of people by giving his professional services free to underprivileged groups, and by serving non-professional groups or organizations in a non-professional way, thus ethically advertising himself and inspiring the respect, confidence and liking of a larger number of people through whom future clients or patients may come. Merely belonging to such organizations is not enough; service is what brings success.

STEP III. *Cultivate a strong, enduring, acceptable, dominant emotion which will DRIVE you, regardless of the work involved, the sacrifices, disappointments and discouragement, constantly forward, for year after year, on the path you have chosen, which will never let you rest until your purpose is achieved.*

Without such a driving power, Steps I and II, and all other steps, will be like New Year's resolutions, entered upon with enthusiasm, but soon forgotten or neglected. Only such a driving power can give you the utmost efficiency, prevent the constant vacillation which causes inefficiency, inspire you to make your own program and follow it, to think day and night until the necessary ideas are forthcoming, the necessary means and plans, the required effort and application, with which no mere book, nothing else in all the world, can provide you. WITH such a driving emotion, you will FIND YOUR OWN WAY TO SUCCESS, you will never rest until you do; and you will need neither my help nor anyone else's. WITH such a driving emotion, you will discover for yourself what to do, and you will do it WITH such a driving emotion, barring ill health and other unforeseen handicaps, you will GET RICH IN SPITE OF YOURSELF.

Though envy, revenge, and many other emotions occasionally serve as the driving power for more or less limited success, the only generators of success worth considering in most cases are the six which I have discussed in this book.

1. Greed or lust for power. 2. Fear of poverty. 3. Pride.
4. Love of work. 5. Love of people. 6. Love of God.

The first three are not recommended. Be careful not to choose one of them until you have seriously considered my warnings about them. I do recommend the fourth, but it has its dangers. The fifth and sixth are recommended with qualification, and are attended by no dangers whatever. Chose any one of the last three as YOUR generator of success, and then cultivate it.

Most readers, because of their reluctance to accept the practicality of idealism, will probably start with No. 4. When they experience difficulty in maintaining the emotion, they will try No. 5. It is easier to love your work if you love the people that work serves. But for people who take their religion seriously, or who can learn to do so, No. 6 is the best choice. People are far from perfect, and it is difficult to continue loving them without the enduring inspiration of religion. Religious people should find it easy, for the sake of their God, to love people, and for the sake of both, to love their work of service to their fellow-men. Thus the three highest and most powerful emotions are UNITED in driving them to success, and all other emotions either collaborate or become subordinate to that truly sublime combination. Inefficiency no longer plagues them, because they are no longer pulled this way and that, their purposes constantly changed by conflicting and alternating moods and emotions. I do not mean that you must become religious in order to achieve success; but I do say, if you ARE devout, you are foolish not to apply your religion to your daily work, not to use the emotional power it can generate. In fact, I do not see how you can be truly religious without loving people and without desiring to serve them always in a bigger and better way. It is the only way you can carry your love of God into action.

But the non-religious, in many cases, will find the double combination of love of people and love of work equally as effective as the triple combination just discussed. They, too, can thus make themselves completely efficient; they, too, care havo forvoncy, spirit, fire, industry, unswerving determination, courage and faith, driving them constantly and always in the direction of success.

It may be objected that many idealists are not successful. This is simply because they do not APPLY the-driving power of their ideas to their daily work. They look upon the latter of their ideals to their daily work. They look upon the latter as something apart. They have somehow been given the idea that making money, even through service, is objectionable or sinful, that their job or business is without merit because they get paid for their work. The conflict of emotions aroused by such false ideas causes inefficiency, made worse by the very strength of their ideals. If they will but transmute their daily work into an INSTRUMENT, a FULFILLMENT of their ideals, they will be blessed with an efficiency never before experienced. When the Bible speaks of the difficulty of rich men getting into Heaven, it is probably speaking of the rich of that day, most of whom gained their wealth through other people's losses, through conquest, chicanery, DISservice. There were few PRINCES OF SERVICE then, except for prophets and spiritual leaders. But in modern America we DO have princes of service, people who have made their wealth ONLY by ADDING to the security, comfort and happiness of their fellow-men. Today these rich men are our BEST SERVANTS. And theirs is the reward promised in the parable of the talents: "To him that hath shall be given."

STEP IV. Find a means for renewing your zeal, whenever it lags.

Some will find this means in inspirational books and lectures, others in religious books or sermons. Some will find it in music, others in contact with the people they serve. Some will find it in trade, technical, or business magazines and books. And others will be inspired by the example of other men in their field of effort, or other men in other fields. The public libraries are full of biographies which can be helpful in this direction. YOUR means depend upon your psychology, and must be found by yourself.

STEP V. If your zeal still should lag, ponder seriously whether you are in the right vocation. If not, find another in which you can serve with more enthusiasm and spirit.

If necessary, the change is worth the sacrifice; but try all the other steps before giving up the skills you have already acquired. Here you must be on your guard. The other fellow's pasture always looks greener. But if you definitely and permanently dislike your work, then almost any change is a change for the better. For great success, love of work is a main essential. Look to your hobbies, your avocations, for suggestions as to the field of work you should select. (For other suggestions, I recommend the classified telephone directories of large cities.)

STEP VI. When you finally rise to a position of authority, either in your own business or another's, employ men who can teach you something, men who have learned elsewhere, or promote men in your own organization who have had the alertness to learn or acquire skills beyond what you have taught them. Thus OUTSIDE ideas and training can be added to yours.

Hiring the other fellow's experience is the shortest road to success. But be sure he has had the experience, and has been successful in the exact work for which you employ him, or in kindred work. Some of the greatest successes I know of do not have too much ability. Some have had little education. But they do know how to select and handle men with experience to do much of their work for them.

As an advertising man, I have often been amazed at the lack of wisdom shown by business men in employing advertising agencies or advertising managers. They select a general practitioner when they could just as easily hire a specialist in that particular field. One might as well hire the family doctor to fill one's teeth. The family doctor can learn to fill teeth; but why pay for his education? The general practitioner can lose a lot of money for his client before he can avoid the mistakes which the specialist will avoid from the beginning. Employ specialists, whenever possible. It may mean the difference between success and failure; and at the least, will save much money.

Having employed the specialist, you may ALSO employ the general practitioner, as a source of OUTSIDE ideas. The specialist can check these and weed out those which have already been found impractical when applied to this particular field. The general practitioner often does not know that his brilliant idea has already been tried in this field at some time in the past and found wanting. Nevertheless, the general practitioner can often borrow an idea from another field, which has never been tried in the new field, and which is worth trying. To sift the wheat from the chaff, the specialist's judgment is needed. Just because ideas are new does not mean that they are good. Often the public is not ready for new ideas, no matter how good these are.

The same principles hold true, whether you employ a lawyer, an accountant, an artist, or any other professional or executive help. Hire or promote men who can TEACH you, and let yourself be taught. Don't think you know all there is to know about your own business. Men who have had their training only under you and who know only what you know are often invaluable. But you may also need men who may not know as much, but know something DIFFERENT.

Don't let your ego put restrictions upon the service you give to the public. You can never know so much, even about your own business, that there is no more to learn.

All this does not mean that you should obtain your executives from outside your organization. Thoro should bo mcn right m your own plant or office who can teach you something, who have, by keen observation, by burning the midnight oil, by alert study and watchfulness of your competitors, by the reading of business and trade journals, by observation of other fields of enterprise, by their experience before joining you, by self-training, acquired OUTSIDE ideas and training which can be added to yours. They know, not only what you have taught them, but something DIFFERENT which can increase the efficiency of your service, the contentment of your customers and employees, or the breadth of your market. Such employees are rare nowadays. By all means, promote them to the executive positions for which they have qualified themselves. MAKE such positions if necessary. To do so has an inspiring effect upon the other employees, as well as upon the men promoted.

First, however, TEST YOURSELF. Do you give your employees a CHANCE to teach you anything? And, if you employ an outsider, will you LET him teach you? If not, your competitors will soon be forging ahead. By being TEACHABLE, many a simple, unpretentious man has risen to be a Prince of Service.

STEP VII: Return to Step III, and keep on returning to it throughout your life. "And whatsoever ye do, do it heartily, as to the Lord, and not unto men."

THE END

EPILOGUE

Sir Harry H. Johnson, 1910-The Negro in the New World. "Money solves all human difficulties. It will buy you love and respect, power and social standing. With money, you can create armies and build navies; you can control the votes of your-fellow citizens. Fund and shape their educational institutes, conduct a press, overcome disease, make actual the charity of early Christianity, achieve all purposes that are noble, and check the devil at every turn; whether he crop up in the form of alcoholism, disease, intestinal worms, religious intolerance, political oppression, waste of earth's resources, or the misuse of corrugated iron. If you are rich, you can roof your dwelling with tiles of beautiful stone slabs, or wooden shingles; marble your terrace of leaden sheets; if you are poor you must content yourself with corrugated iron and know that your dwelling is a blot on the landscape. The one undoubted solution of the Negro's difficulties through-out the world is for him to turn his strong arms and strong legs, his fine sight, subtle hearing, deft fingers, and rapidly developed brain to making money..."

Made in United States
Cleveland, OH
05 November 2026

47668298R00070